I0513023

Contact details:

Website: http://juliemoselen.com

e-mail: juliemoselen@xtra.co.nz

Photography & Design

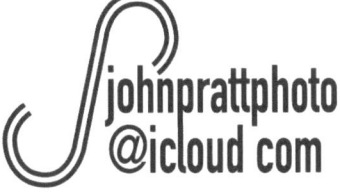

johnprattphoto@icloud.com

© W. John Pratt 2023. All rights reserved. Any unauthorised copying or distribution strictly prohibited

About Julie ...

Julie is a native of Newlyn, in Cornwall, on the Southern end of the Penwith peninsula. Penwith is a rugged slab of granite, soaring more than 60m above the turbulent waters of the Atlantic Ocean. The Southernmost tip of the Penwith peninsula is literally called Land's End. Still Britain's largest fishing port, thanks to a natural reef, residents of Newlyn are only too aware of the very fine edge that separates success from calamity, life from death. It's a rugged landscape, where people live at the mercy of the forces of nature, as brutal as they can be.

There is literally nothing standing between the people of Penwith, and the traverse of the sun and moon over the horizon. In ancient times, Cornwall was knows as "Bolereon," Greek for "place of the sun." The panoramic views of the horizon and the open sea atmosphere create a unique lightscape which has drawn artists to the area for many years.

Behind and to the North of Newlyn, the Cornish landscape bears witness to the ascent of human civilisation.

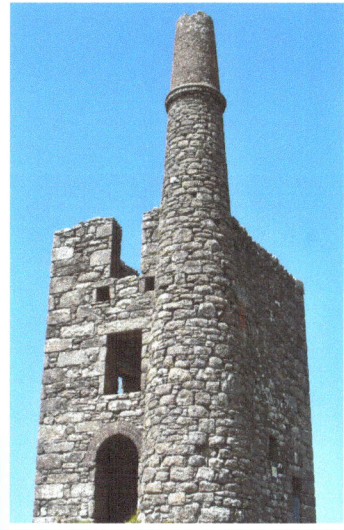

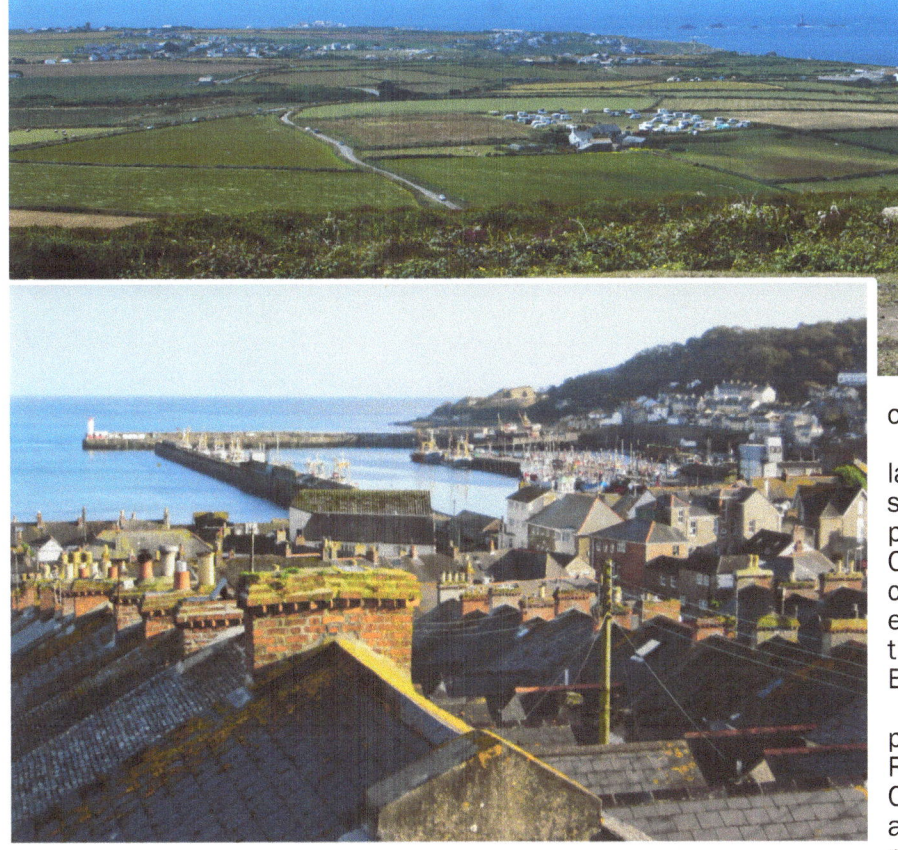

The historic remains of tin mines dot the landscape. Tin mining was a feature of Cornwall since before recorded time. Based on the proximity of Cornwall's mines to it's ports, Cornwall was readily able to export it's tin and copper, and quickly developed an industrial economy in the emerging Bronze Age. Cornish tin and copper have turned up throughout Europe, among the remnants of the Bronze Age.

It was that flourishing mineral economy that placed Cornwall at the heart of the Industrial Revolution. Driven by demand for metals, Cornish inventors and innovators developed and perfected the steam engines and pumps, mining machinery and railway locomotives, fueling the transformation of the World.

(Top Right) Ding Dong mine pump house. (Centre) Looking South-West over Penwith to the Atlantic ocean. (Above) Newlyn and it's harbour in 2022.

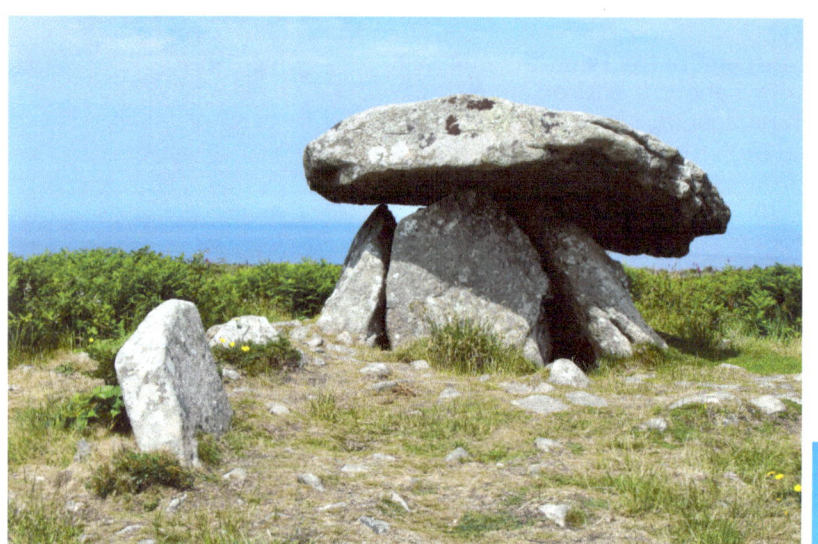

Ironically, few traces of industrialisation remain. The ancient monuments of Neolithic people still predominate across the landscape. Dating back thousands of years, these stone structures are evidence of one of the Worlds oldest civilisations. With each piece of granite weighing several tons, in the context of the times, and of the people that built them, they are literally monumental structures. Over several millennia, these monuments have cast their shadow over the incursion of hostile armies, the rise and fall of industry, and the harsh Cornish environment itself.

Growing up in Newlyn, Julie has fond memories of walks on the moors. The passage of time means that

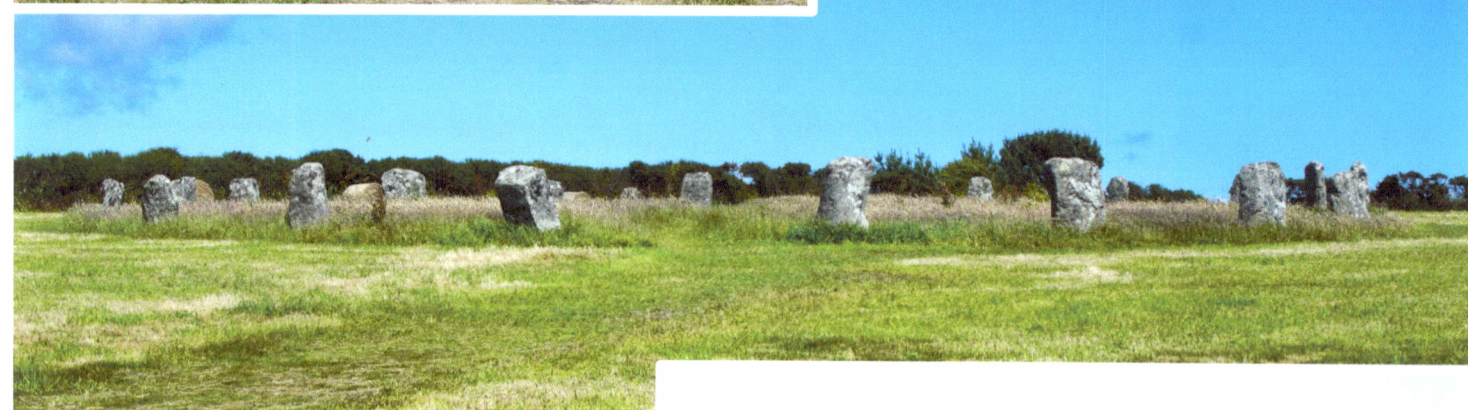

these sites are mostly known only by name. The people that built them left little else behind. Why they built these structures, and how they were built, remain mysteries that have yet to be solved. Their unmistakable and enduring prominence on the landscape speaks to simpler times, simpler communities, and a deeper connection with Mother Earth, and the unique landscape of Cornwall.

It was only after Julie relocated to New Zealand, that she realised the gravitational pull these ancient monoliths exerted on her. From across the World, she studied all the available research into the origins of her people. Who were they? How did they live? What were their values, their beliefs?

The Neolithic people of Cornwall, integrated as they were with the sun and moon, tides and

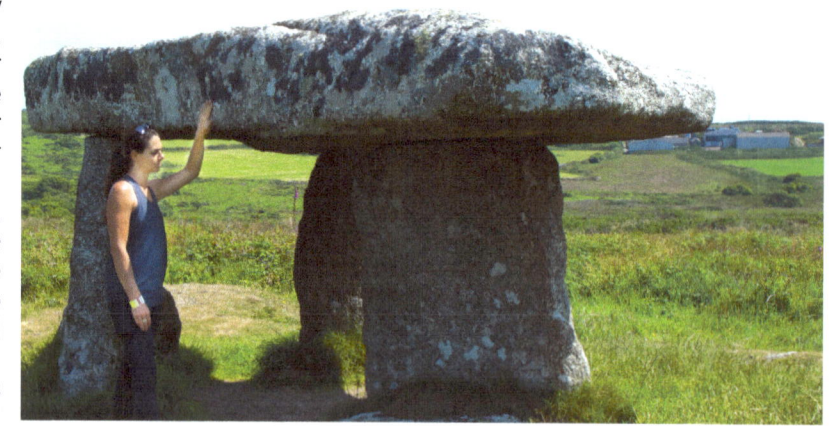

seasons, had gained some knowledge of astronomy. The arrangement of Cornwall's stone circles seems to indicate they were aware of the 19-year Metonic cycle of the sun and moon. The juxtaposition of the stone circles, standing stones, and features of the landscape, seem to define the region, and dynamically respond to seasonal events like the summer and winter solstices.

These elements of the Cornish landscape allude to a sophisticated civilisation, completely attuned, and living in harmony with the environment in which they flourished. Those principles resonated deeply with Julie, who has a heartfelt affinity with Cornwall and the people. Julie writes, *"This idea of sacred space, illumination and alignment fascinates me and is a concept I wish to explore in detail. There is something intriguing about the felt experience of these sacred spaces and how the symbology of such places seems to resonate on a deeply intuitive, subconscious almost subliminal level. There is an energy, frequency or vibration that creates the duality of both awe and fear similar to that witnessed when entering a cathedral. It is this numinous, 'beyond language' experience that I would like to investigate further. How do I convey this same felt perception, intimation and resonance in my sculpture? How can I illustrate the concept of sacred space in my work?"*

It was working at the Newlyn Art Gallery that exposed Julie to art world, and on leaving college she enrolled at the Falmouth School of Art, with the intention of studying photography. It was during her foundation year at Falmouth that Julie was exposed to working with metal, and sculpture, and realised straight away that was the path she wanted to pursue.

Jewellery instinctively felt like a more secure career option, and Julie next went to the Birmingham School of Jewellery, where she learned the art of fine jewellery, completing her B.A.hons Metalcraft & Jewellery Design at High Wycombe, before departing for a new life on the other side of the World in New Zealand.

While focussing on raising her family, Julie established herself making jewellery, and teaching art in Auckland, New Zealand. She describes her time teaching as, *"a really joyful thing for me to do. I could be creative every day, and it broadened my skill base immensely. It was a really good way for me to practice my own art and creativity on a daily basis."*

Back in St Ives, where she enjoyed first-hand exposure to the work of luminaries like the sculptor Barbara Hepworth and the works of the Tate St. Ives, Julie knew that the ultimate expression of her work would be in sculpture. She regards jewellery as small-scale sculpture, with a lot of limitations; *"It has to be comfortable, it has to fit the body, if it's a pendant it has to sit flat, if it's a ring it has to fit around the finger, if it's an earring it has to hang — so many constraints."*

Eventually Julie discovered Oamaru stone. This white sandstone is ideal for carving, since it's easy to work with using only simple tools. Auckland sculptor Stephen Woodward took Julie under his wing, and developed her stone carving skills, which is when Julie produced her first marble sculpture.

Seeing some of the sketches that Julie was working on however, it was Stephen that first realised she would never be able to realise the forms and concepts that she was developing, in stone.

At that point Julie realised her future lay with steel, and she moved across the Arts Centre Estate to work with sculptor Anton Parsons, who schooled her in MIG welding and working with Corten steel. His advice to her was that her concepts were too complex to be realised in steel at this point in her career however, and she started out developing organic forms such as spirals.

Tired of working in the miniature scale of jewellery, Julie decided her first commissioned work would have to be BIG. Reflecting on that first commission, Julie wanted to make a statement. *"I had to go big or go home."* The piece was a 2.2m spiral, which draws inspiration from Celtic culture. *"It's about infinity, about life and death and the continuity of life."*

After perhaps two years, having accumulated some experience working in steel, Julie embarked on a series of developments of the more complex and ambitious 3D forms that she had long been developing in sketch and maquette form. *"The fundamental concept of all my work is about the continuing life cycles of everything, of night and day, masculine and feminine. I'm trying to demonstrate harmony through the balance of things. For example you can't have light without shadow, so it's only when both are present that a balance exists. It's the same with masculine and feminine. You can't have one without the other."*

Julie continues to explore and develop concepts of harmony, balance and continuity in her sculpture. *"Trying to find the essence of that feeling is what I'm trying to do in my work. Articulating that in words is incredibly difficult. Trying to articulate that in 3D is easier."*

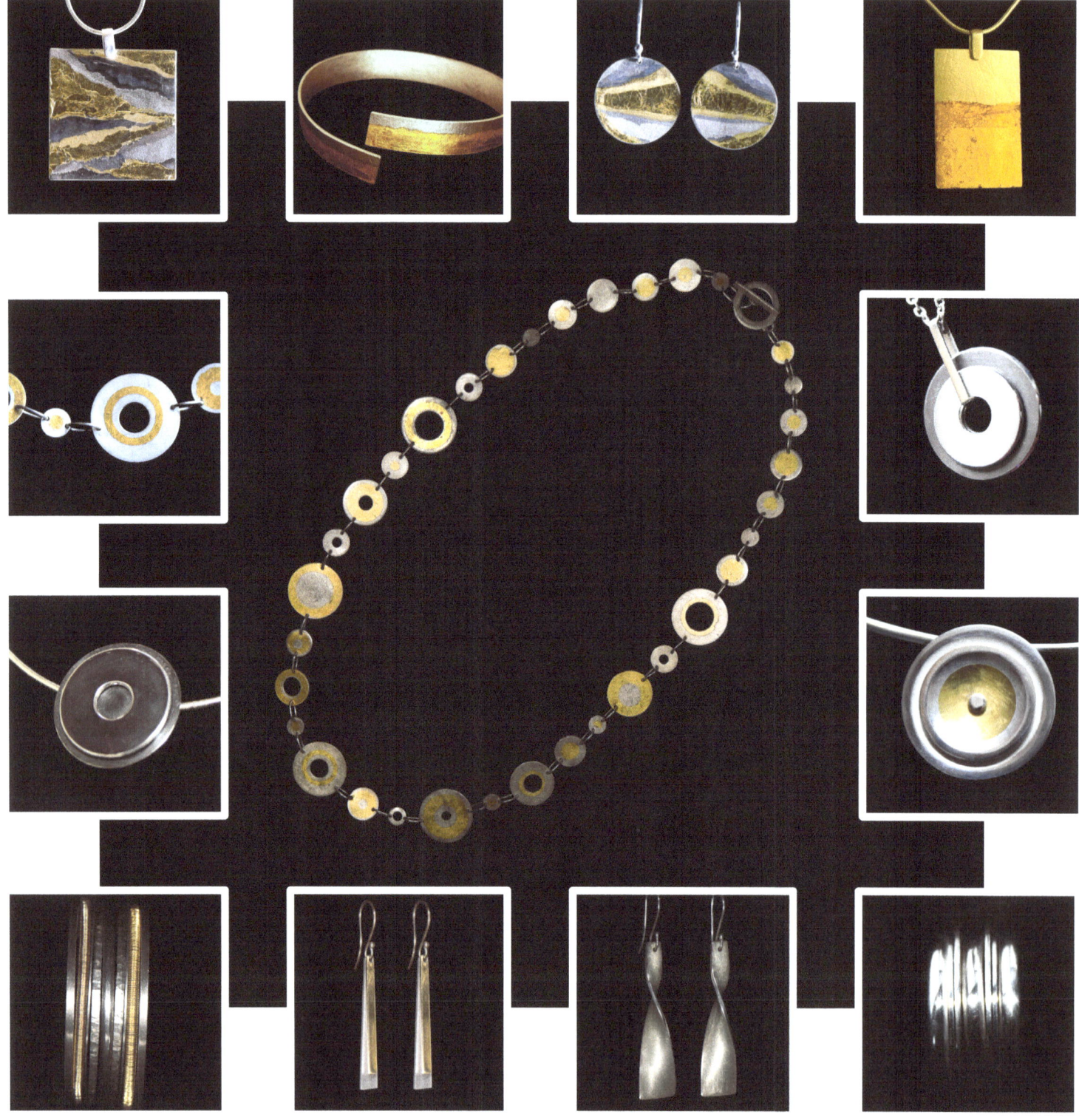

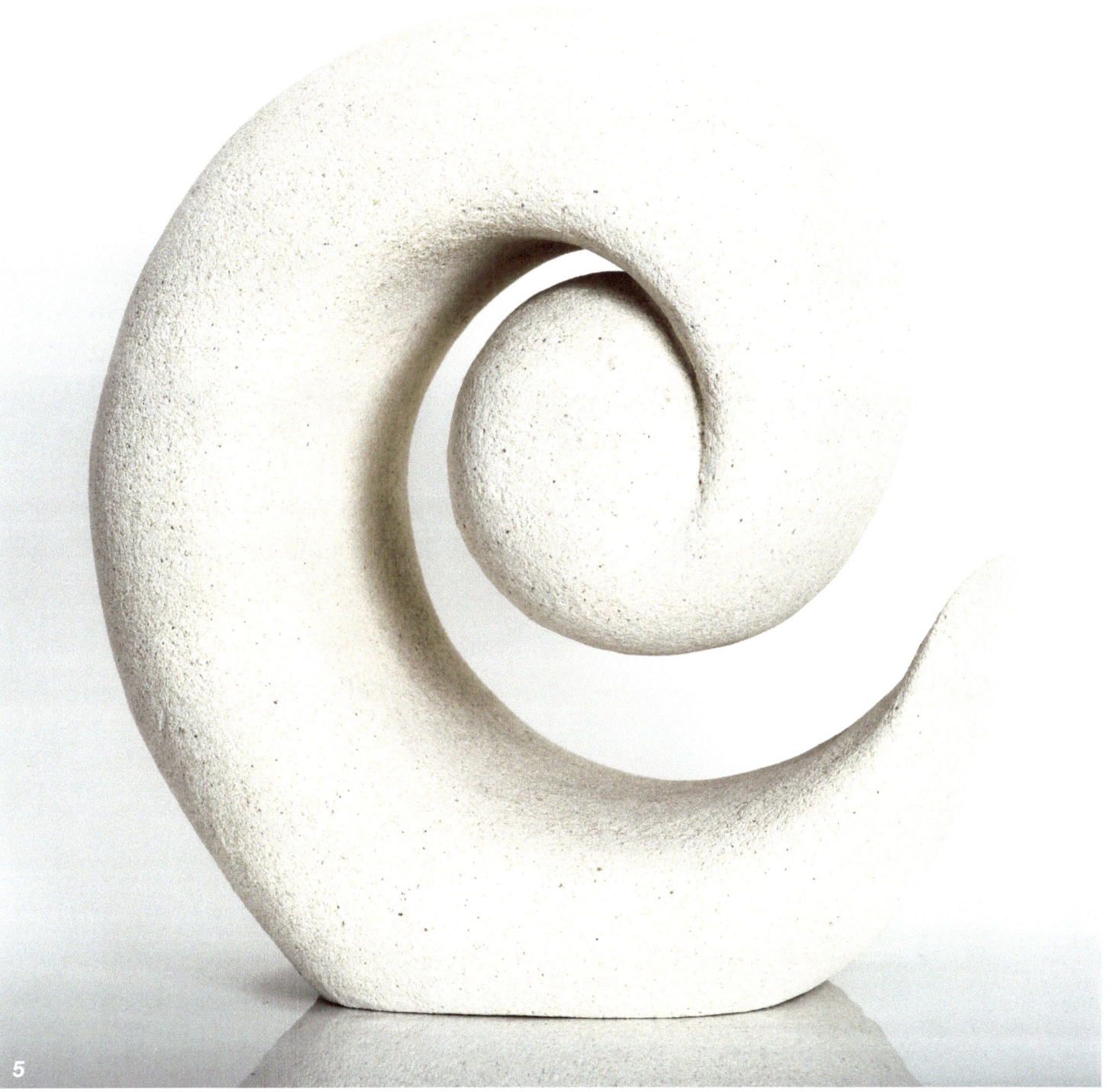

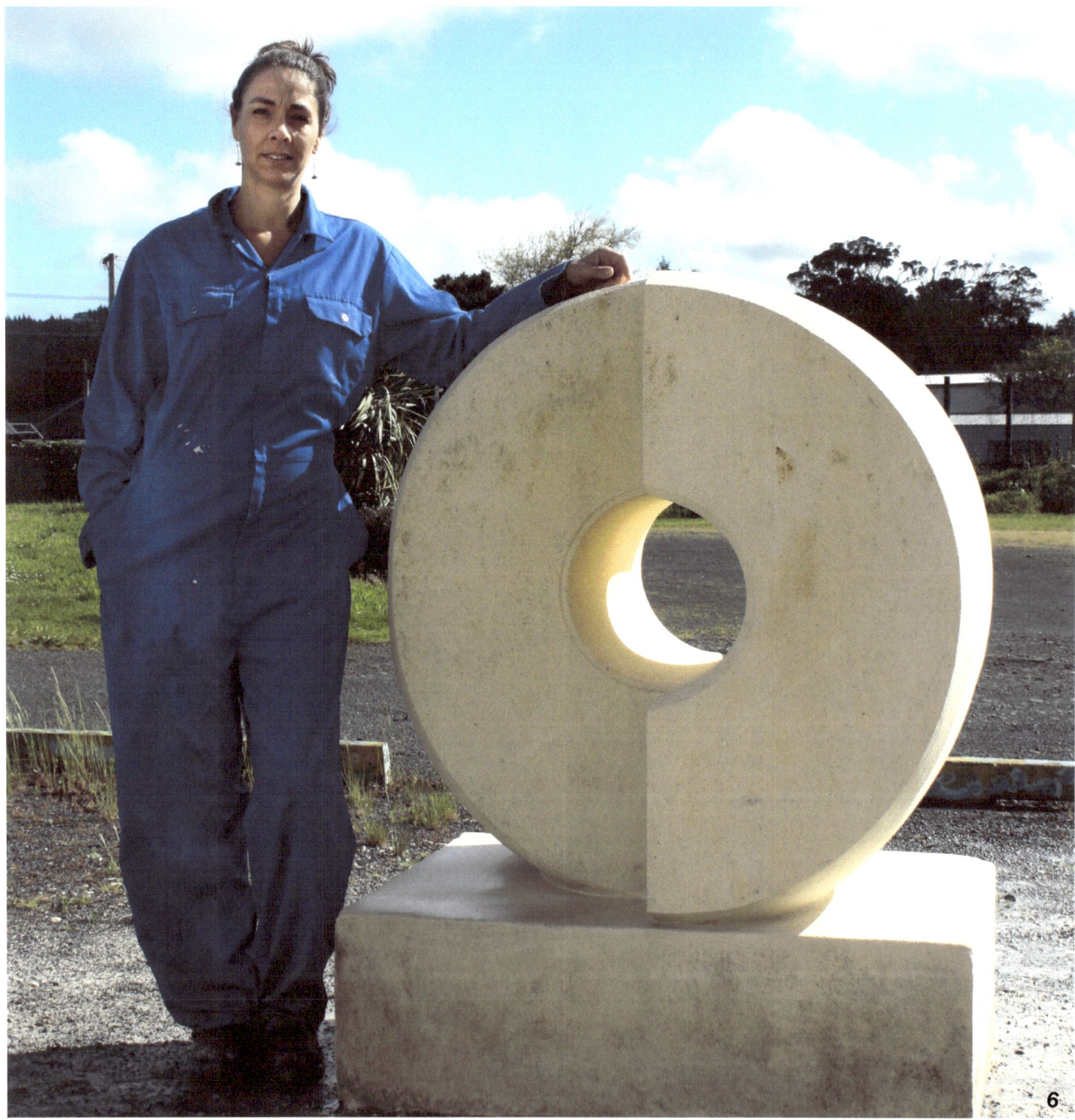

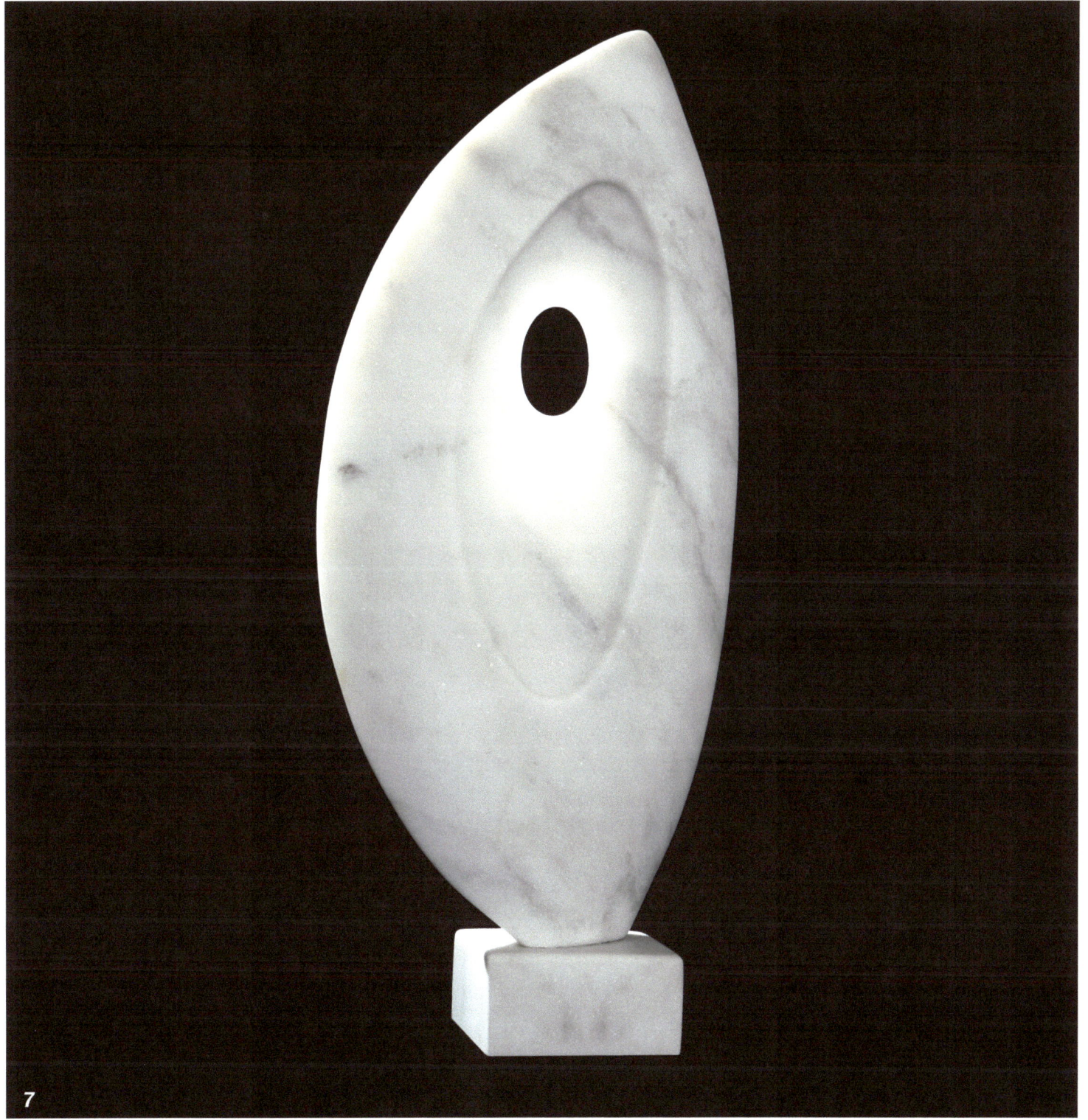

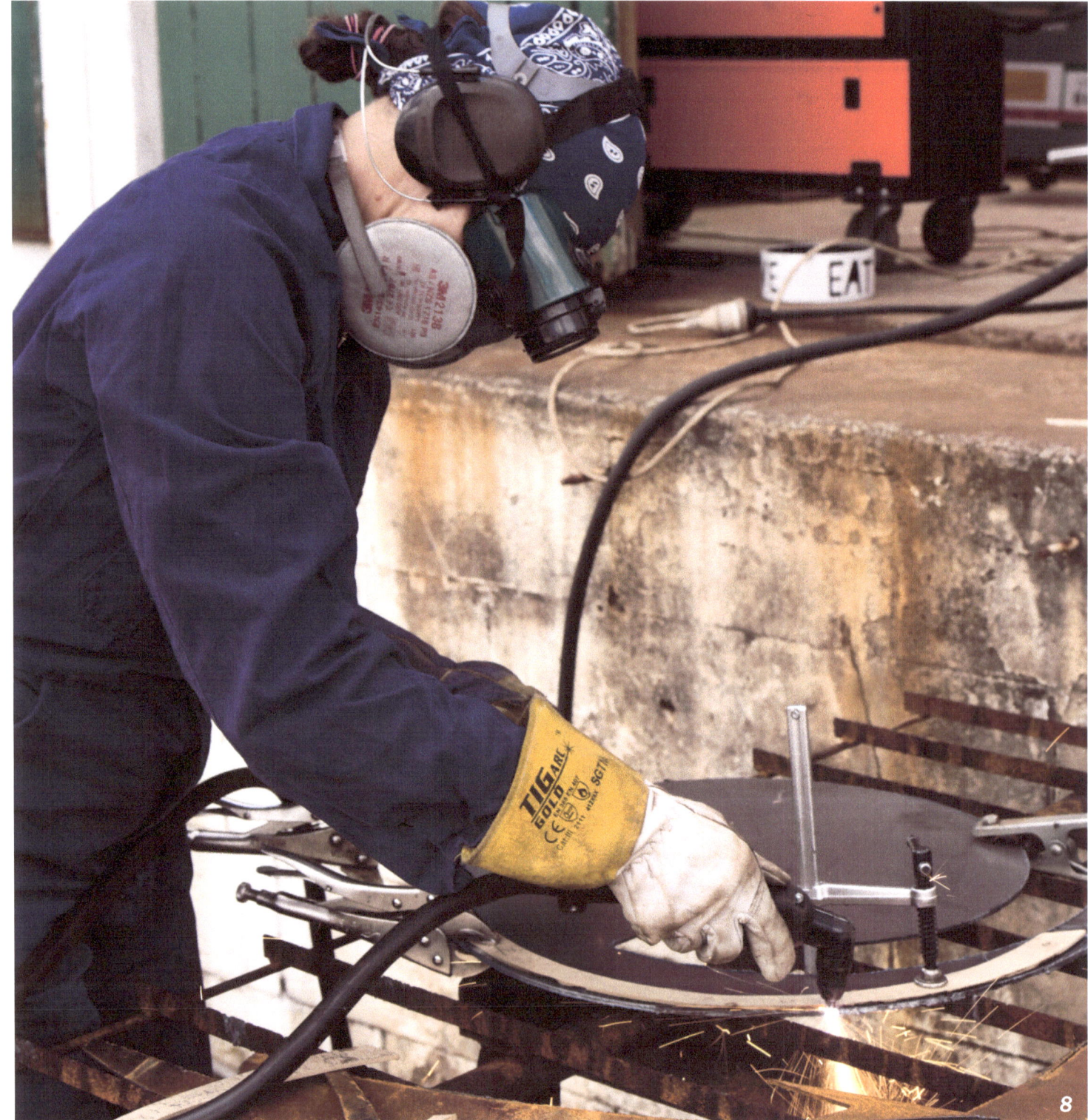

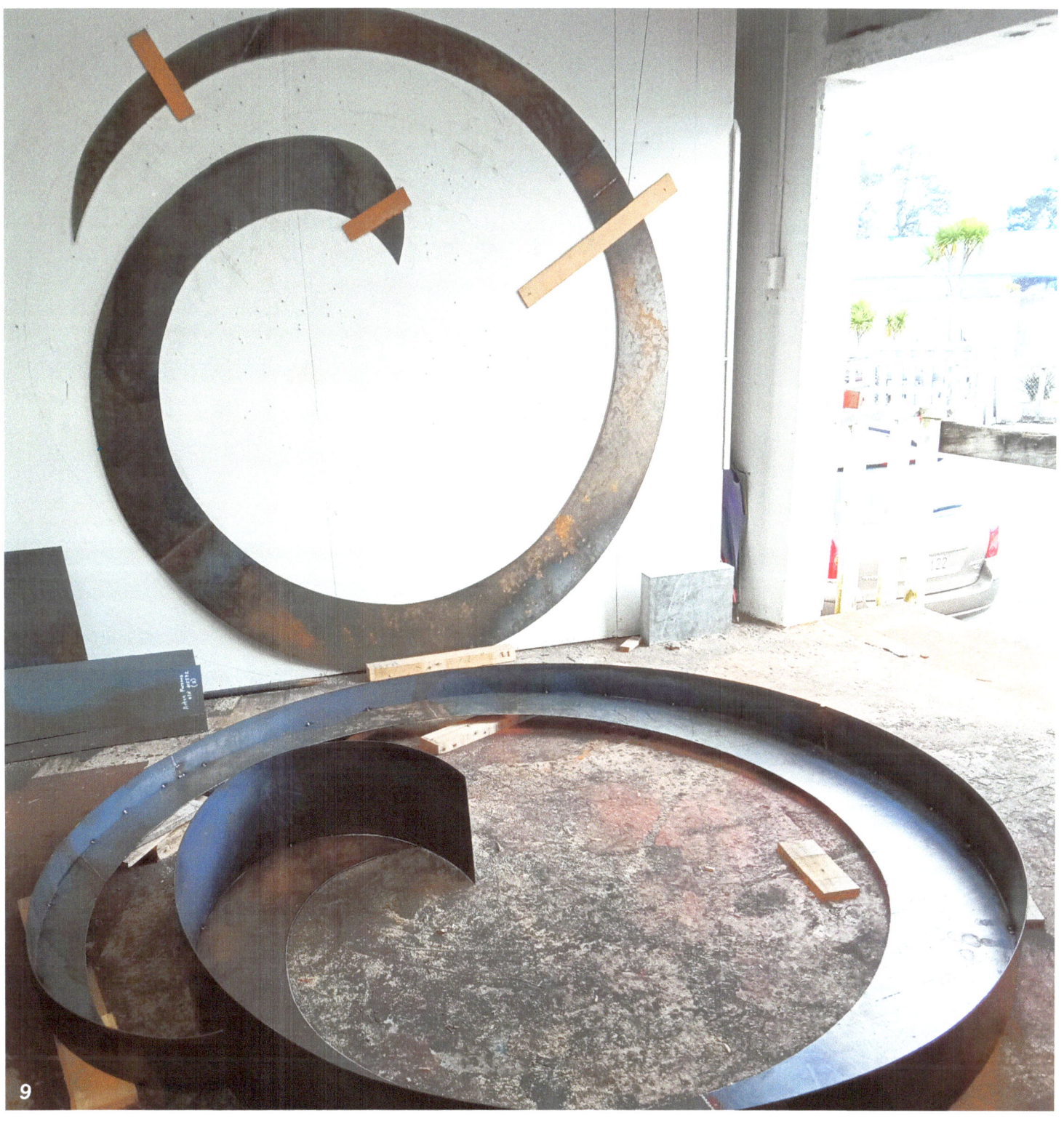

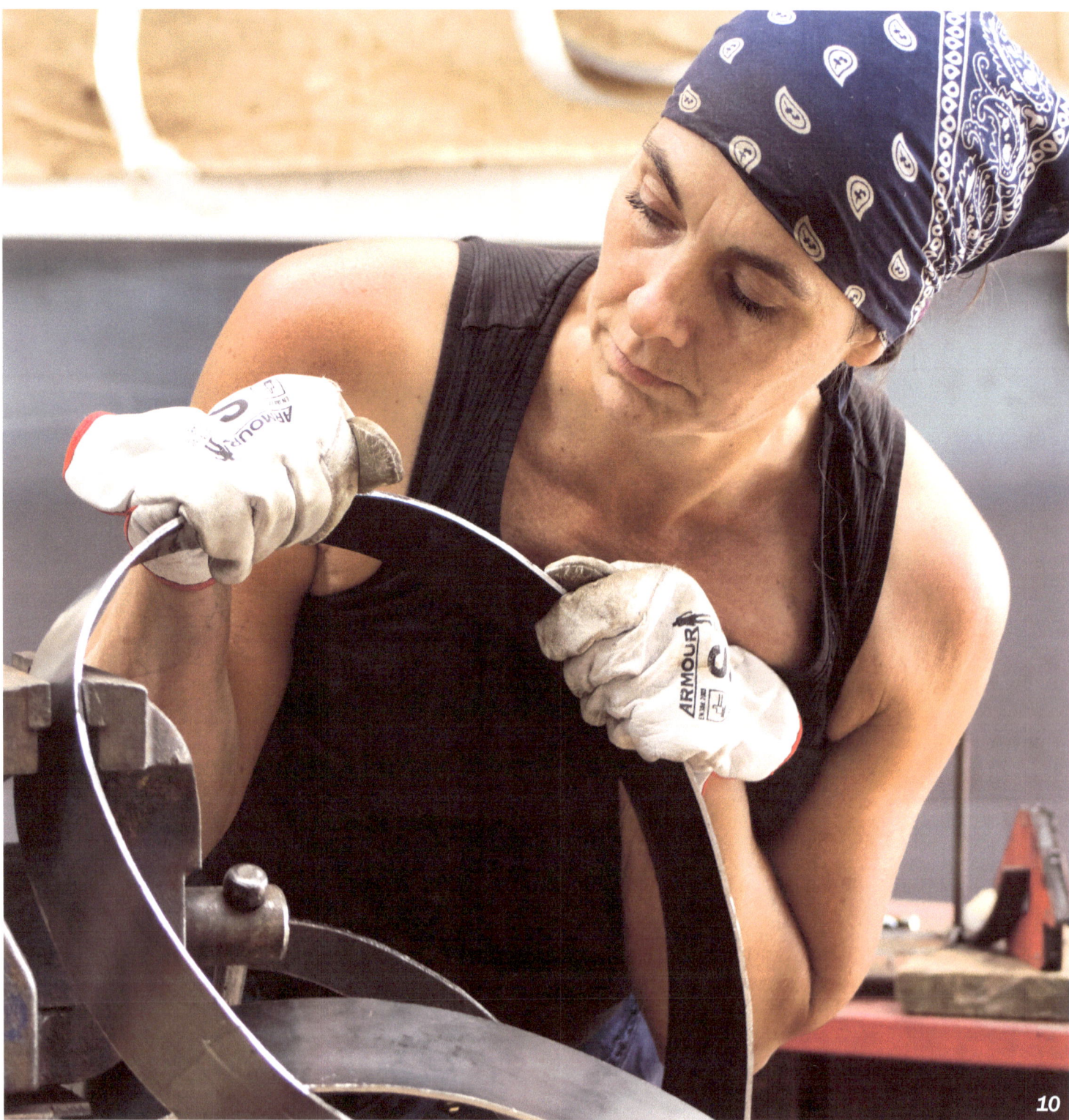

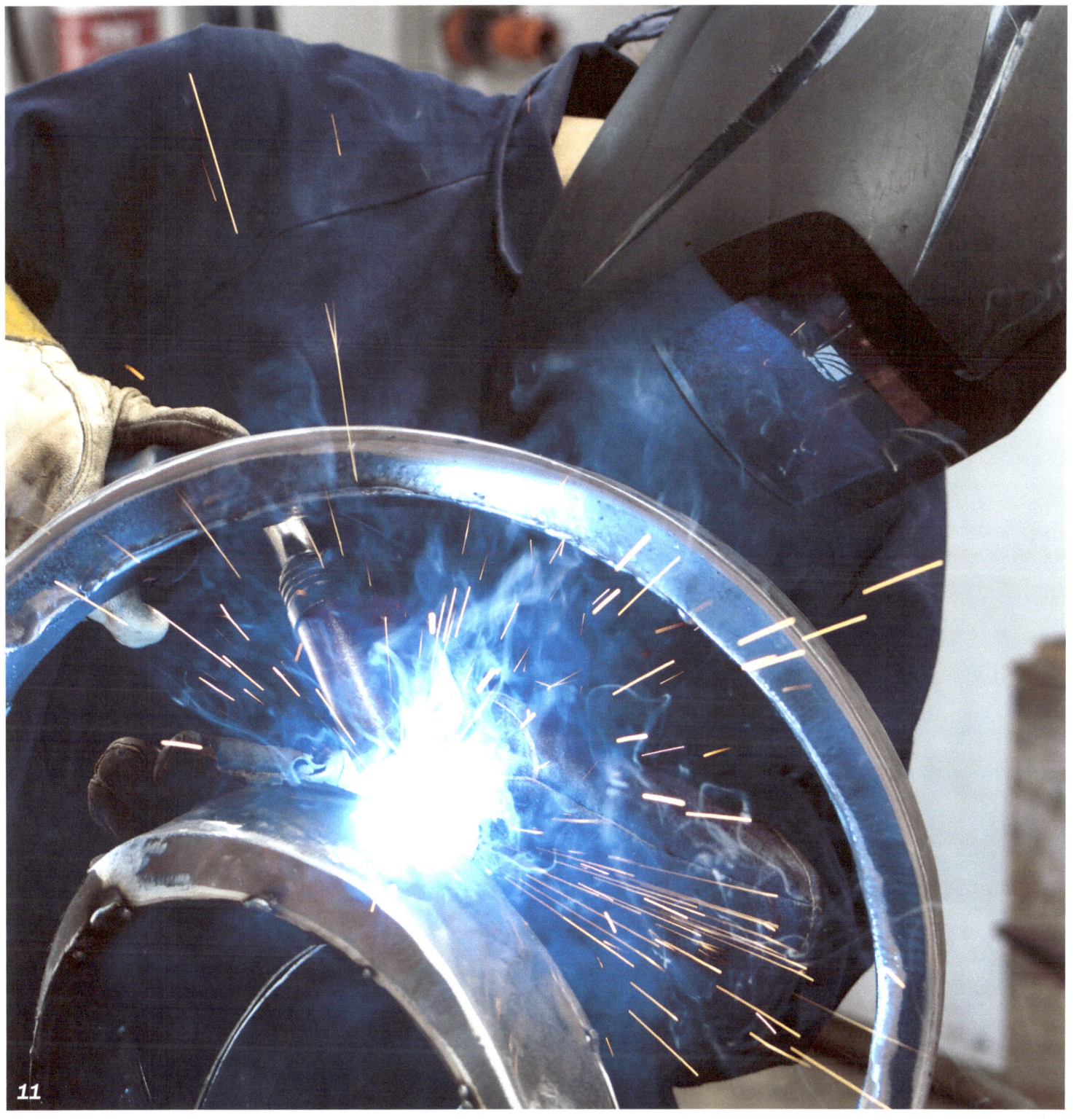

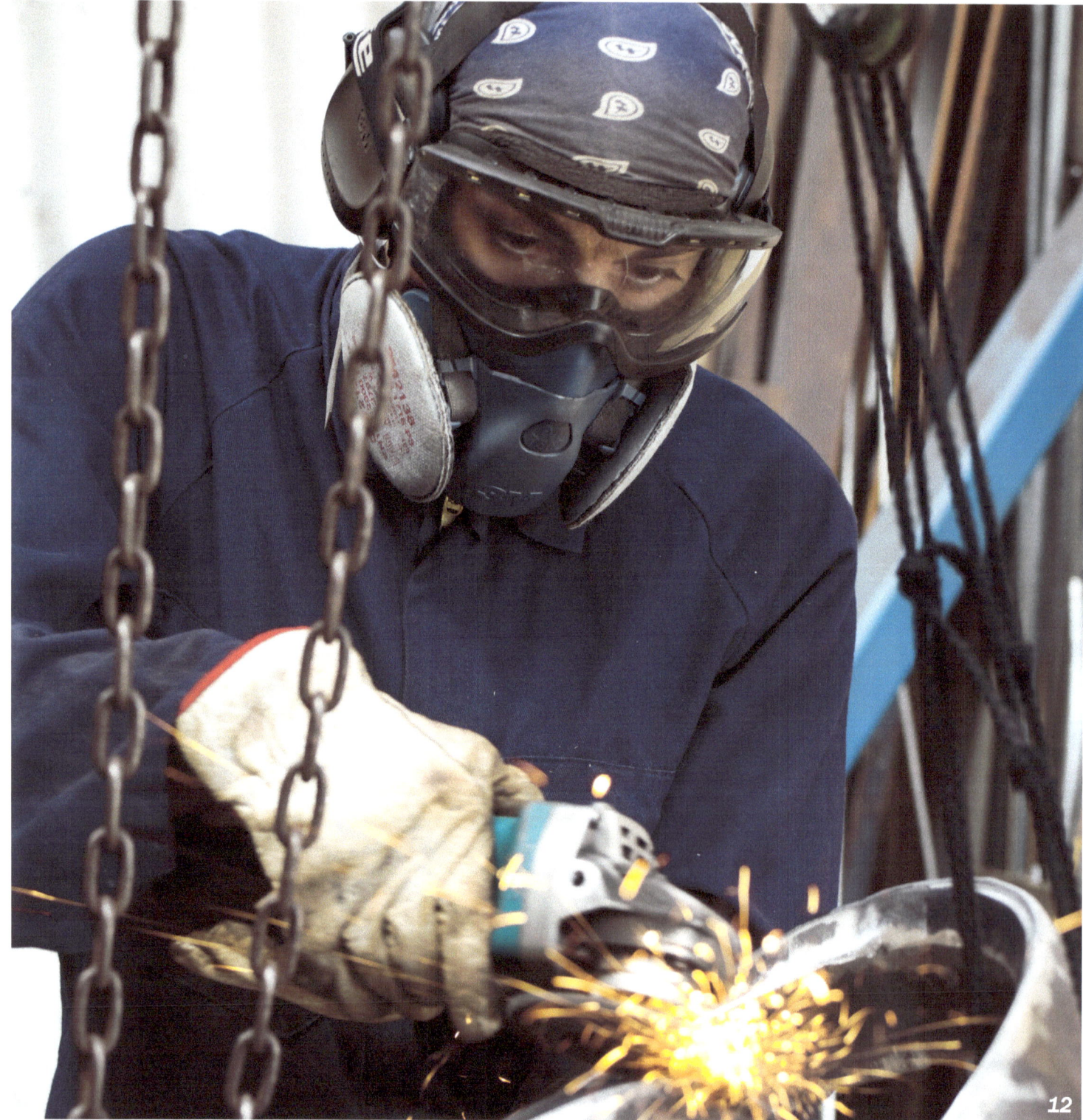

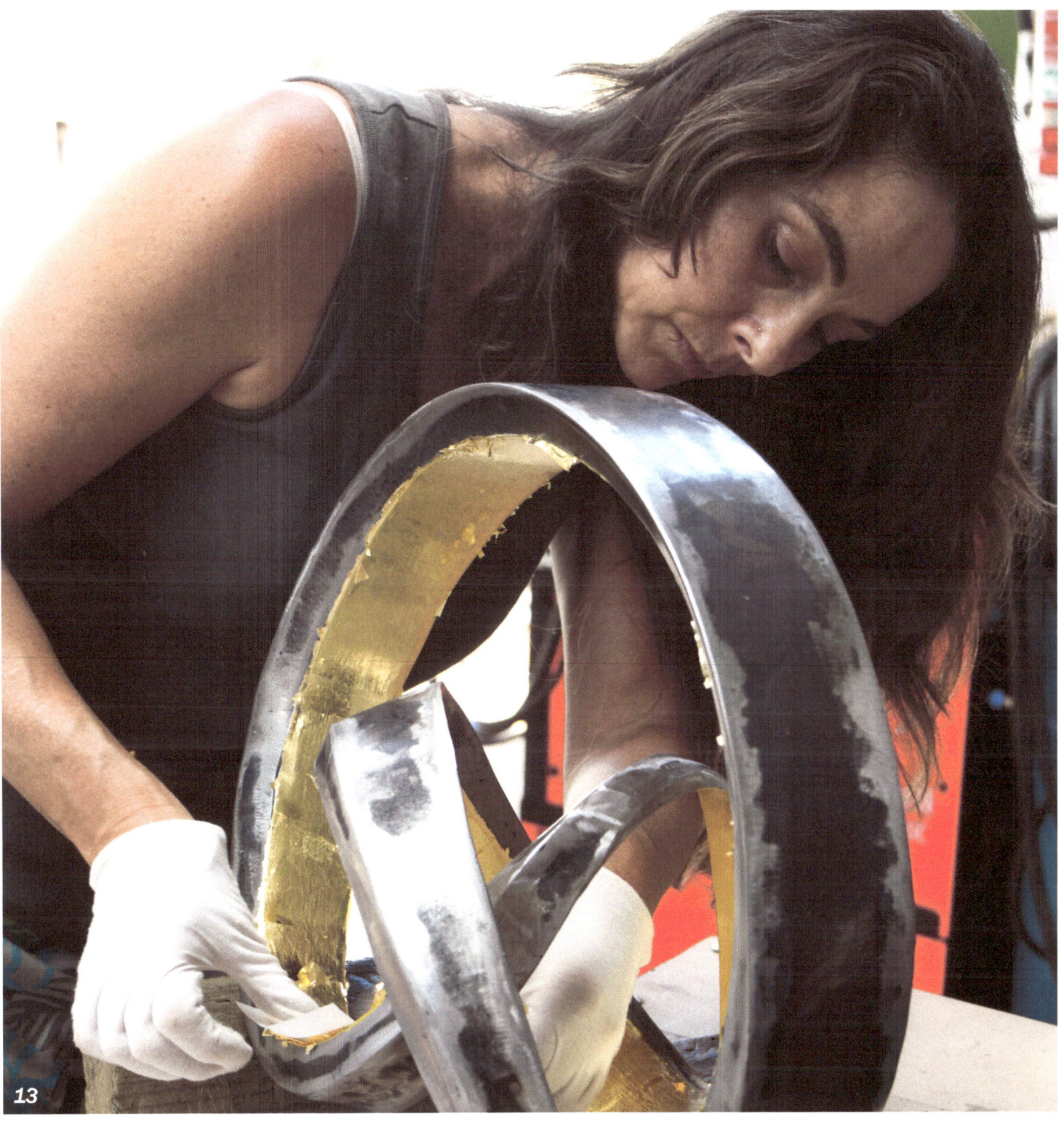

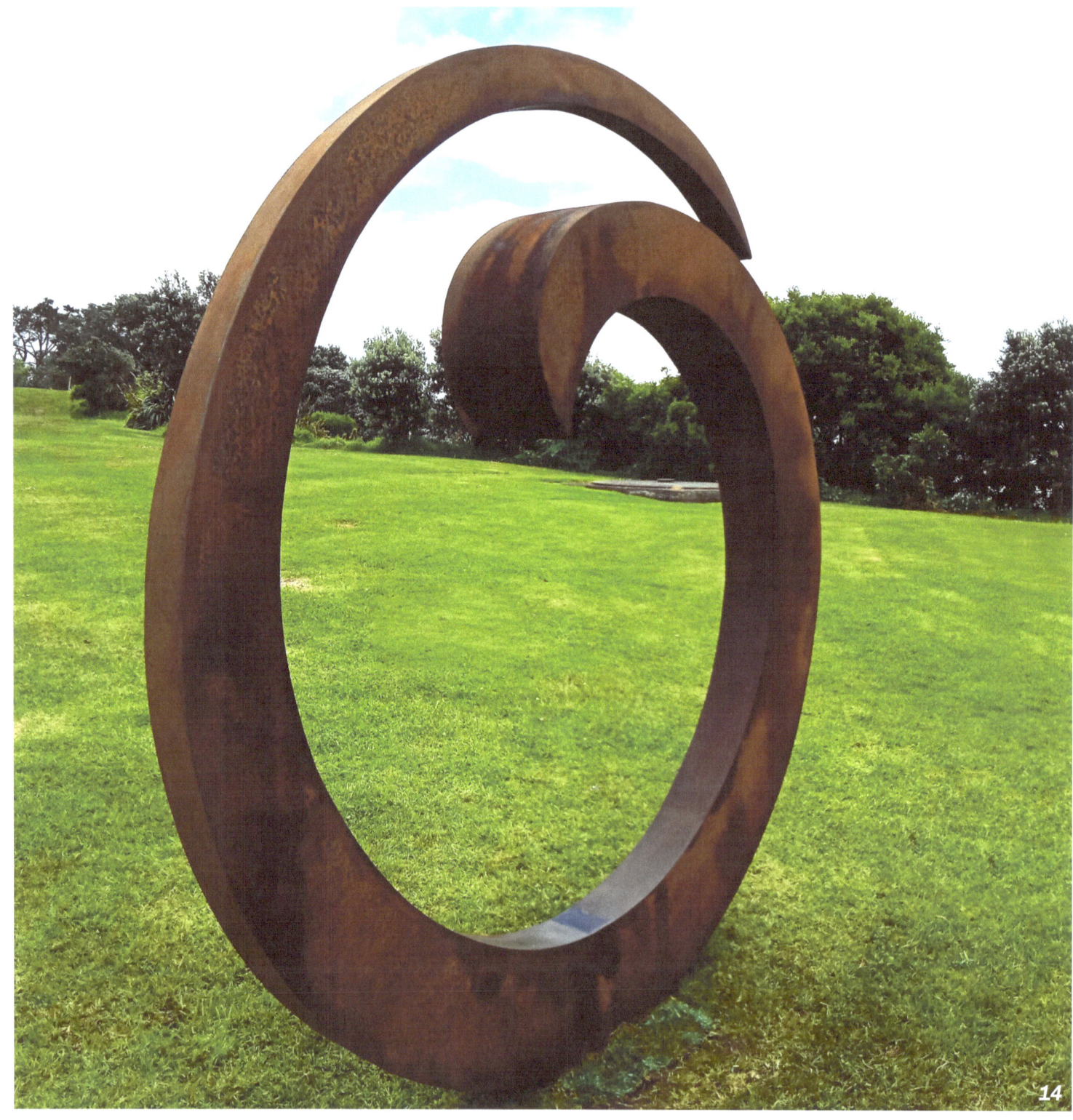

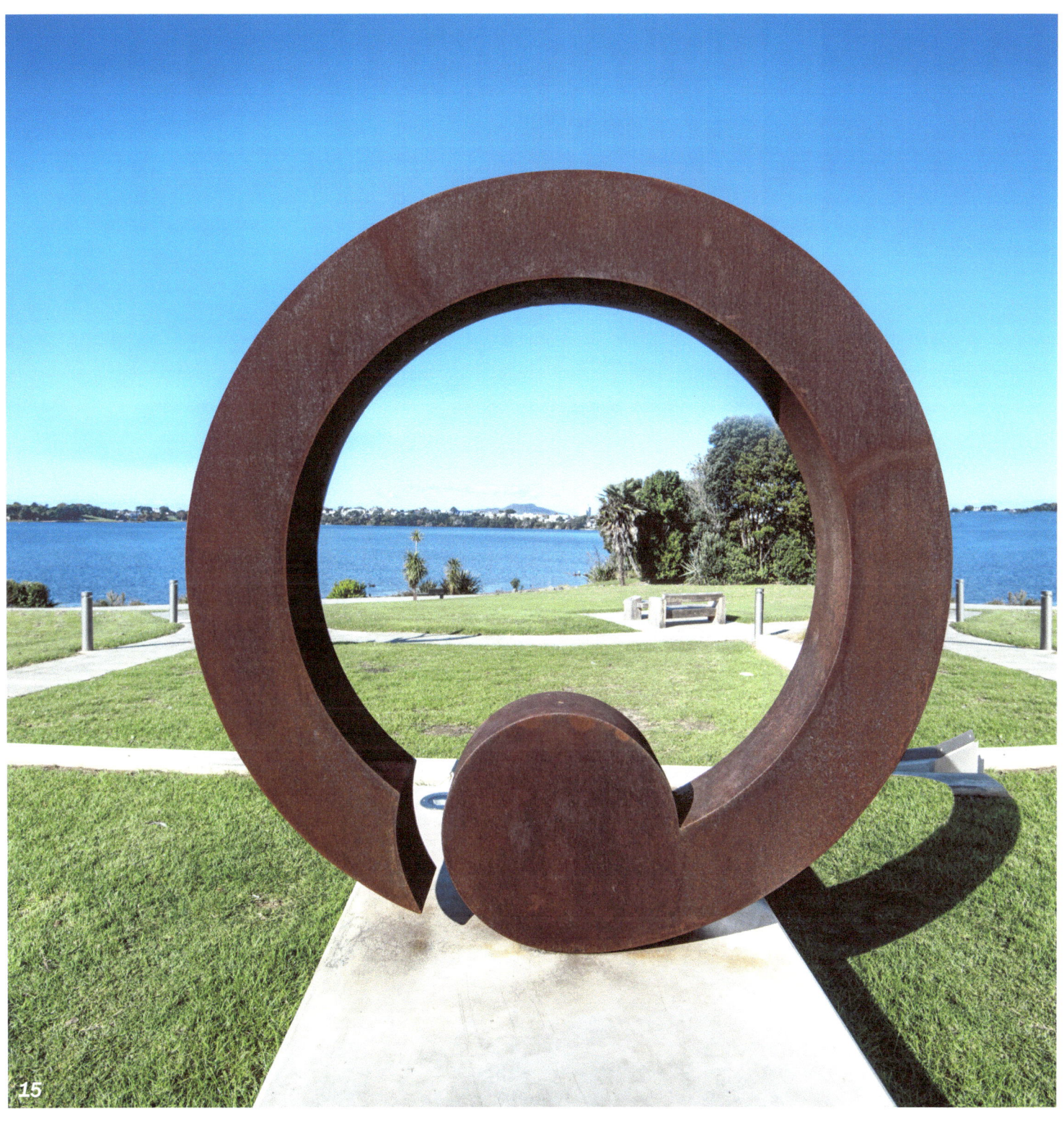

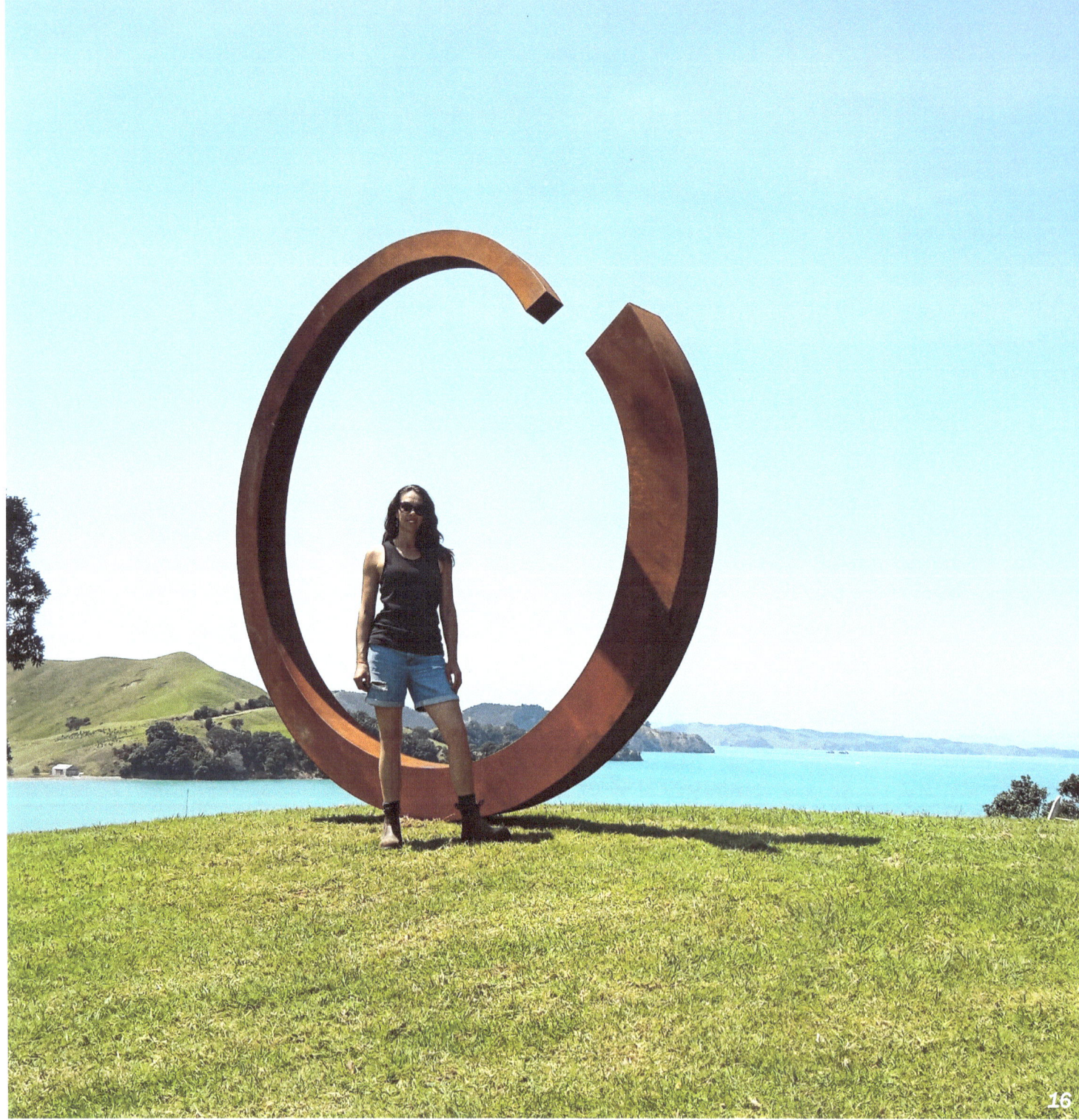

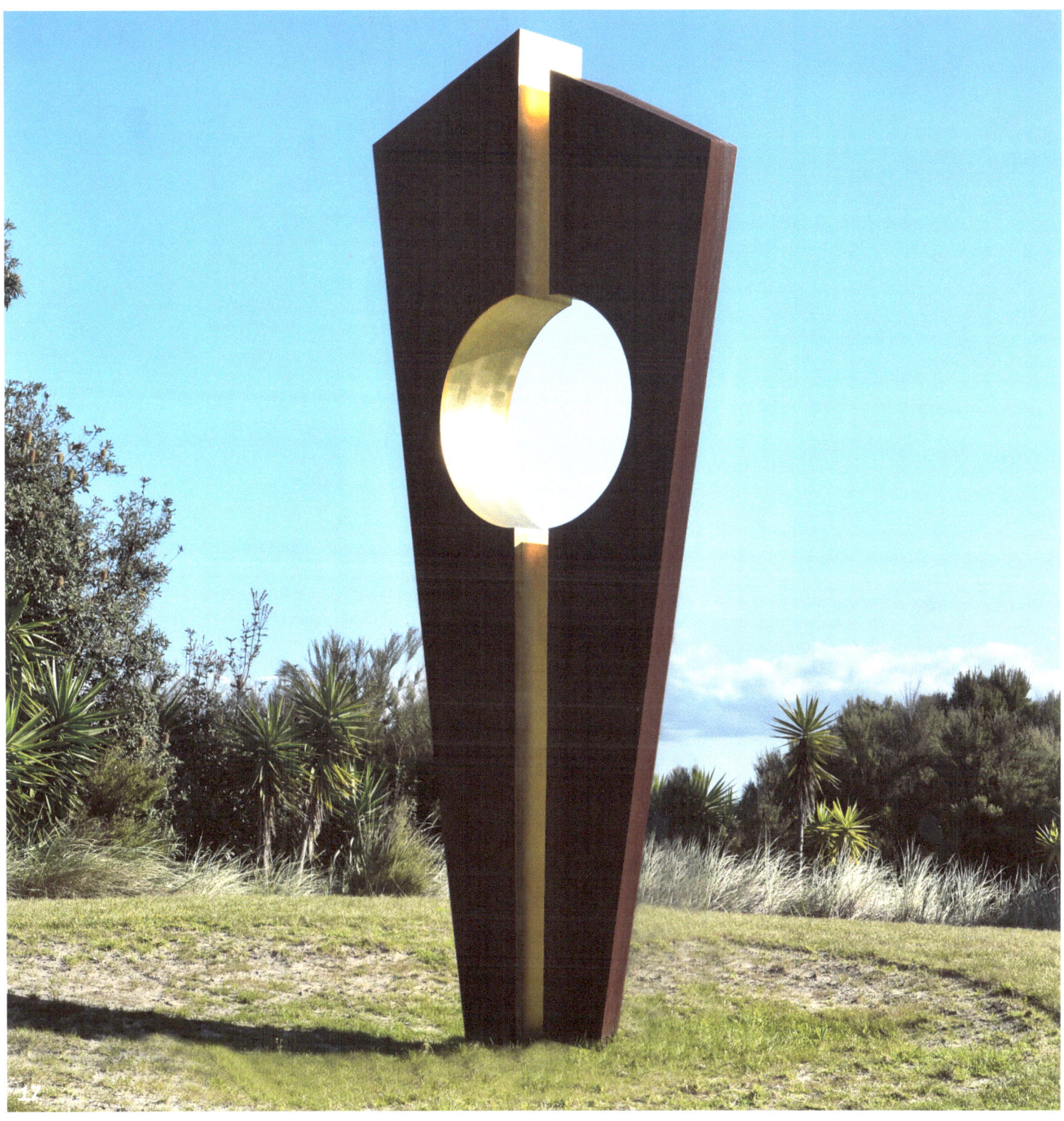

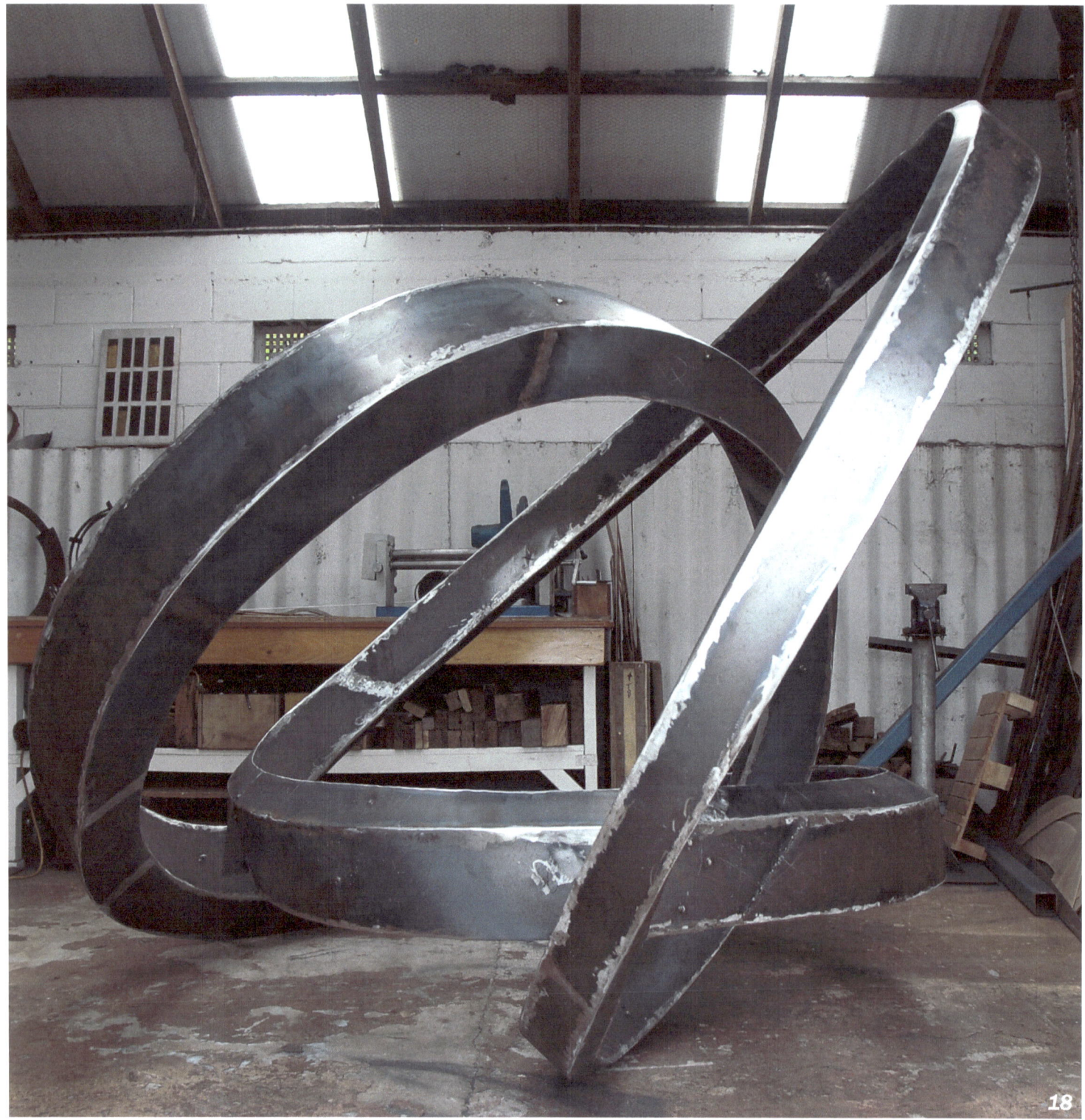

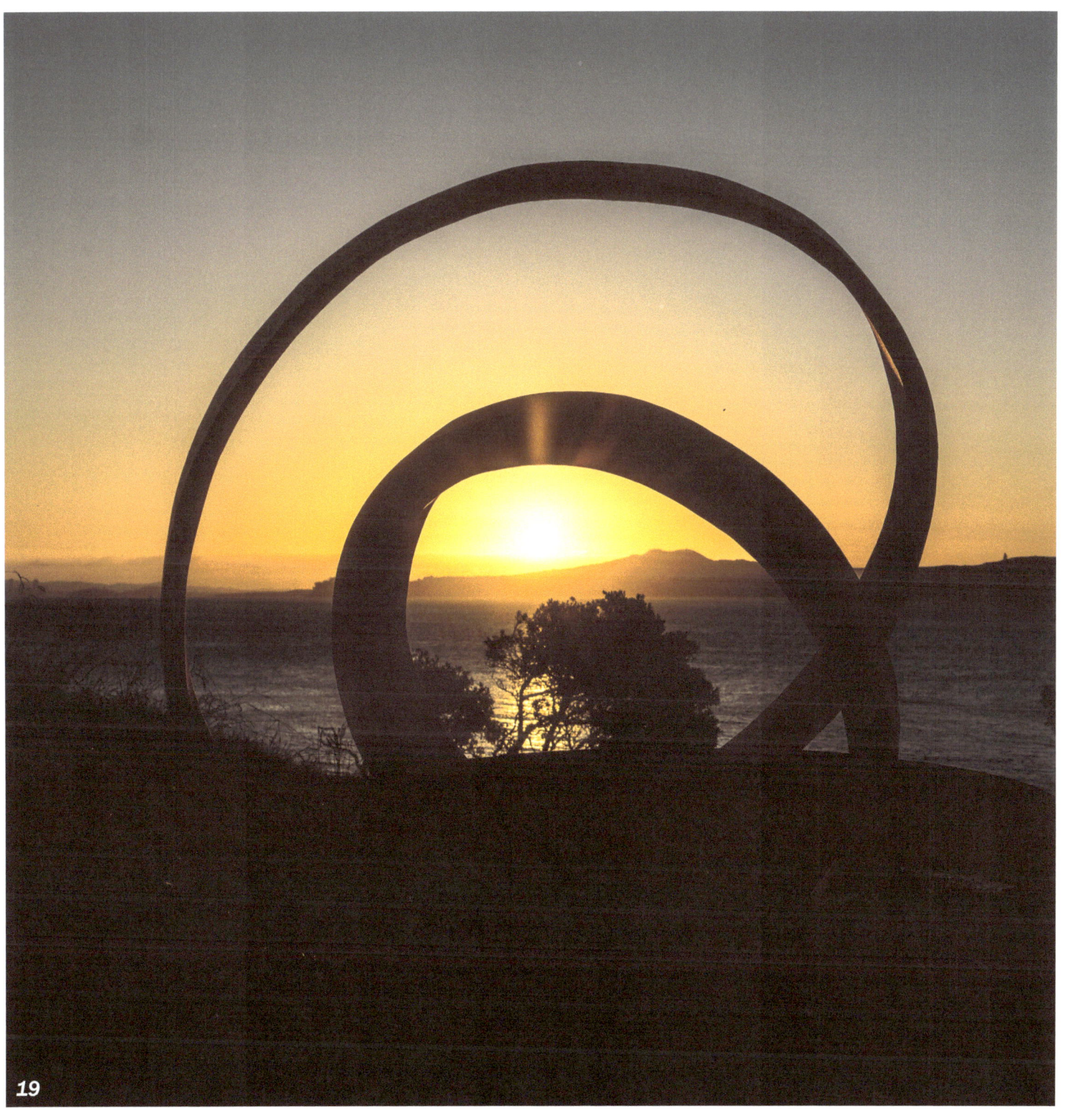

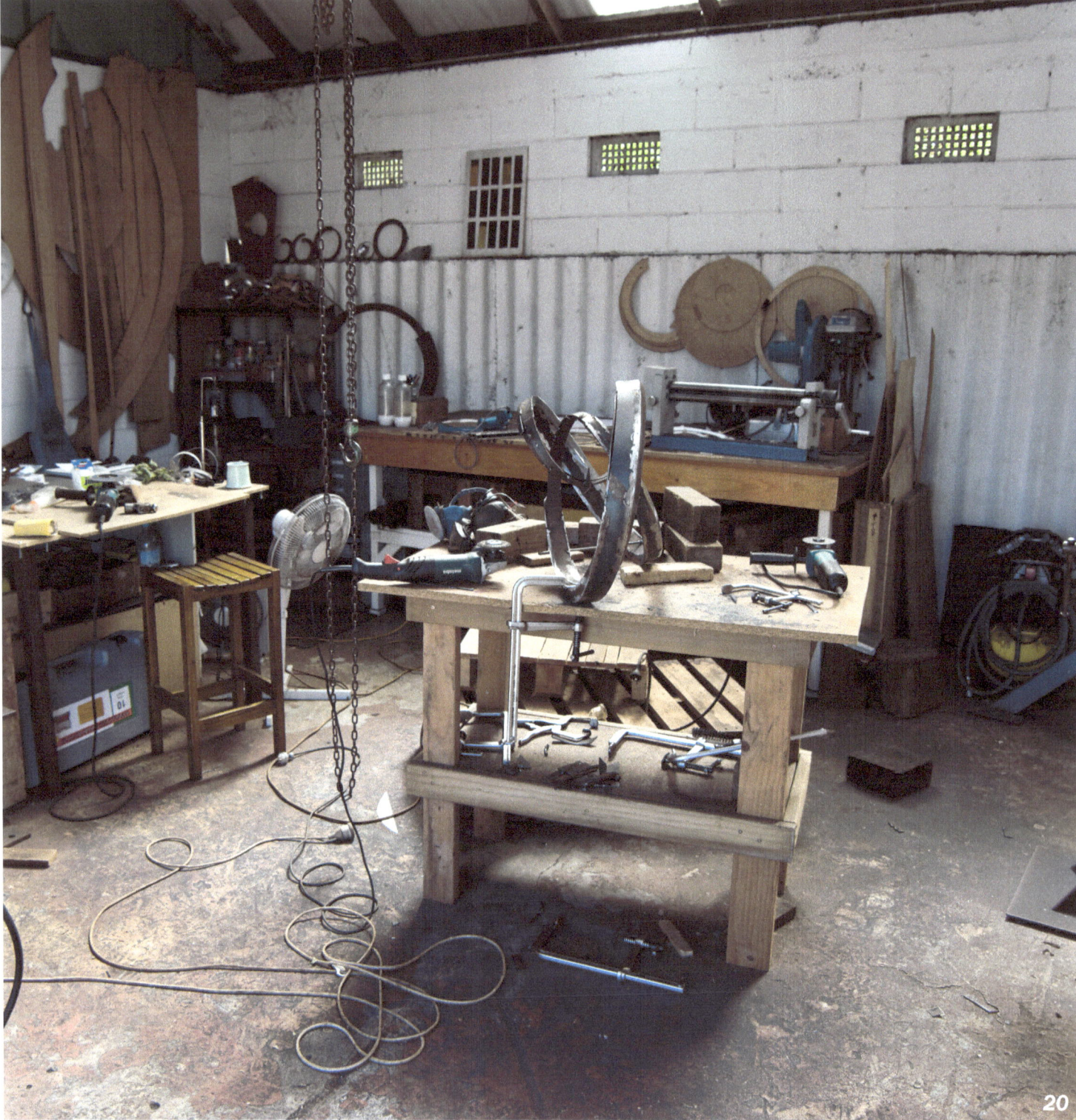

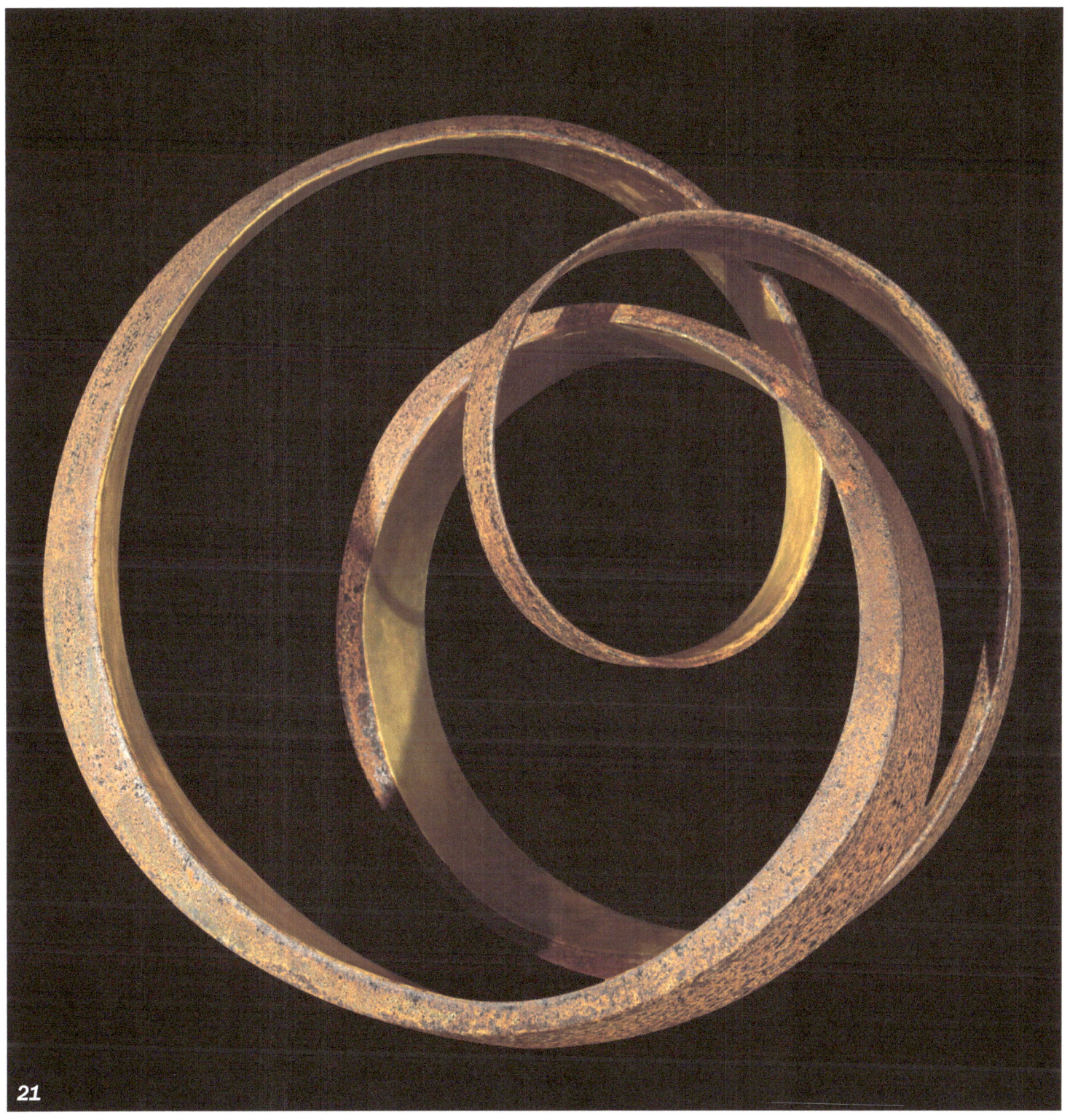

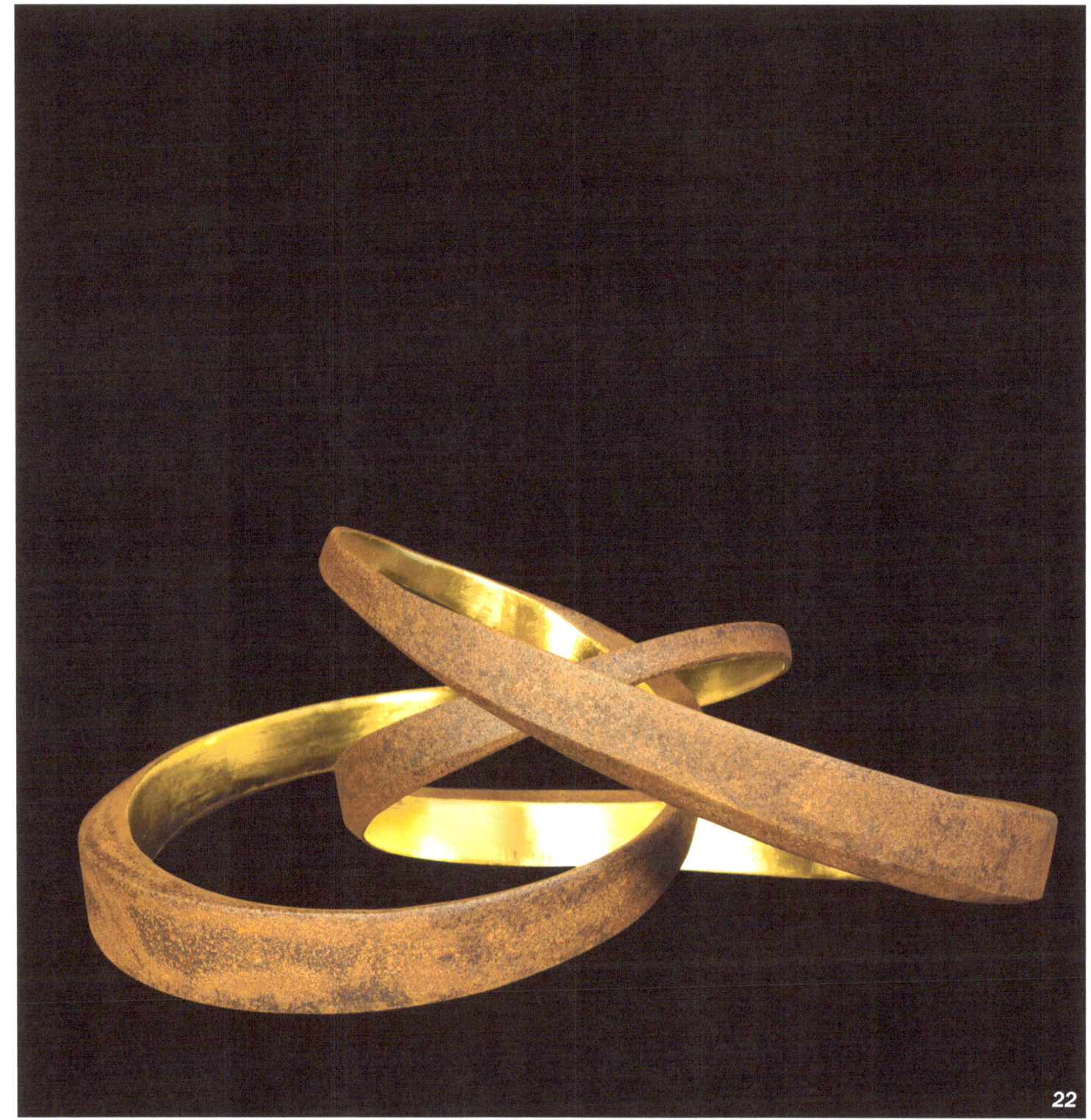

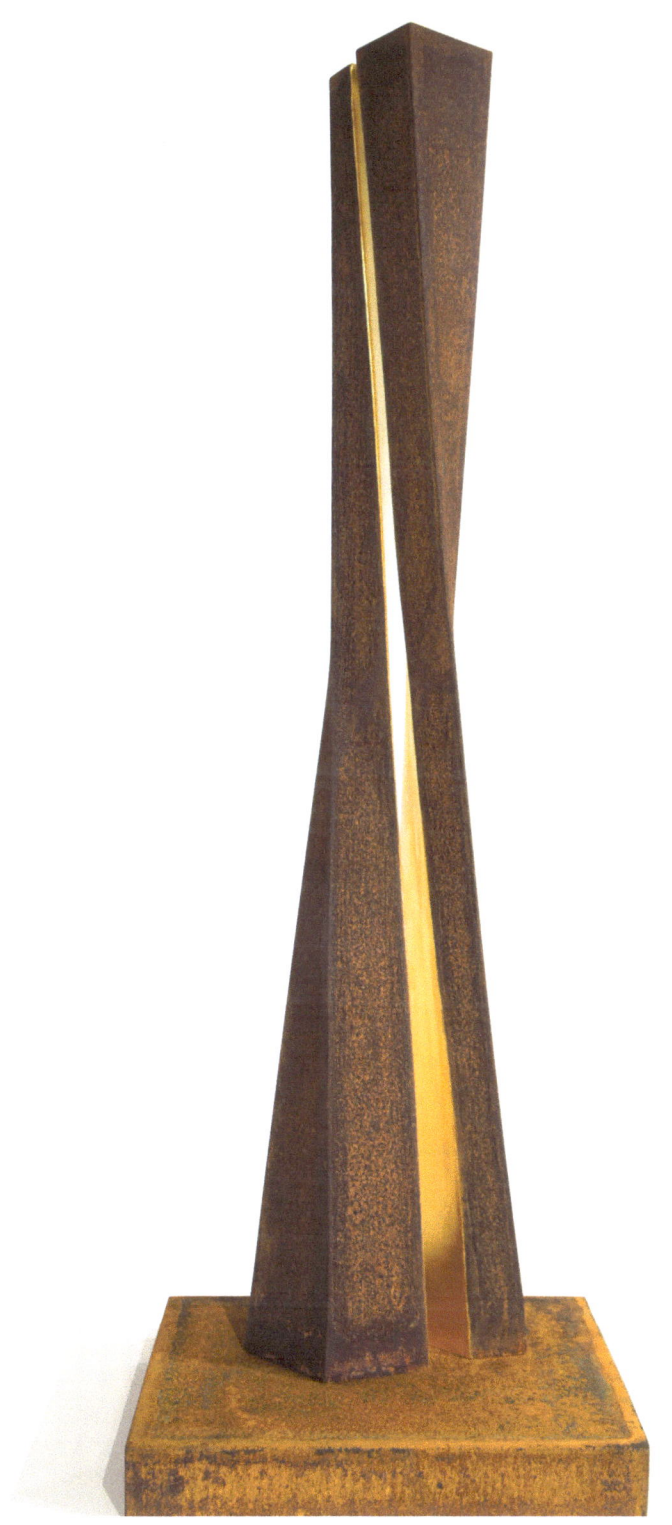

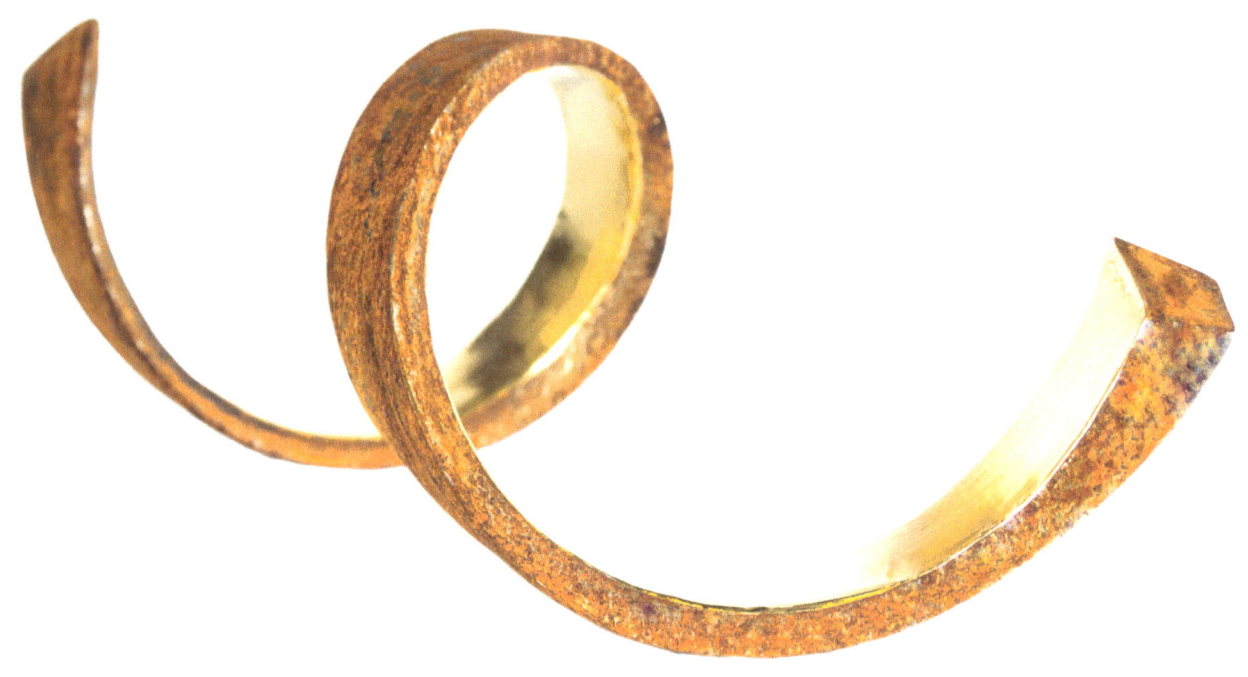

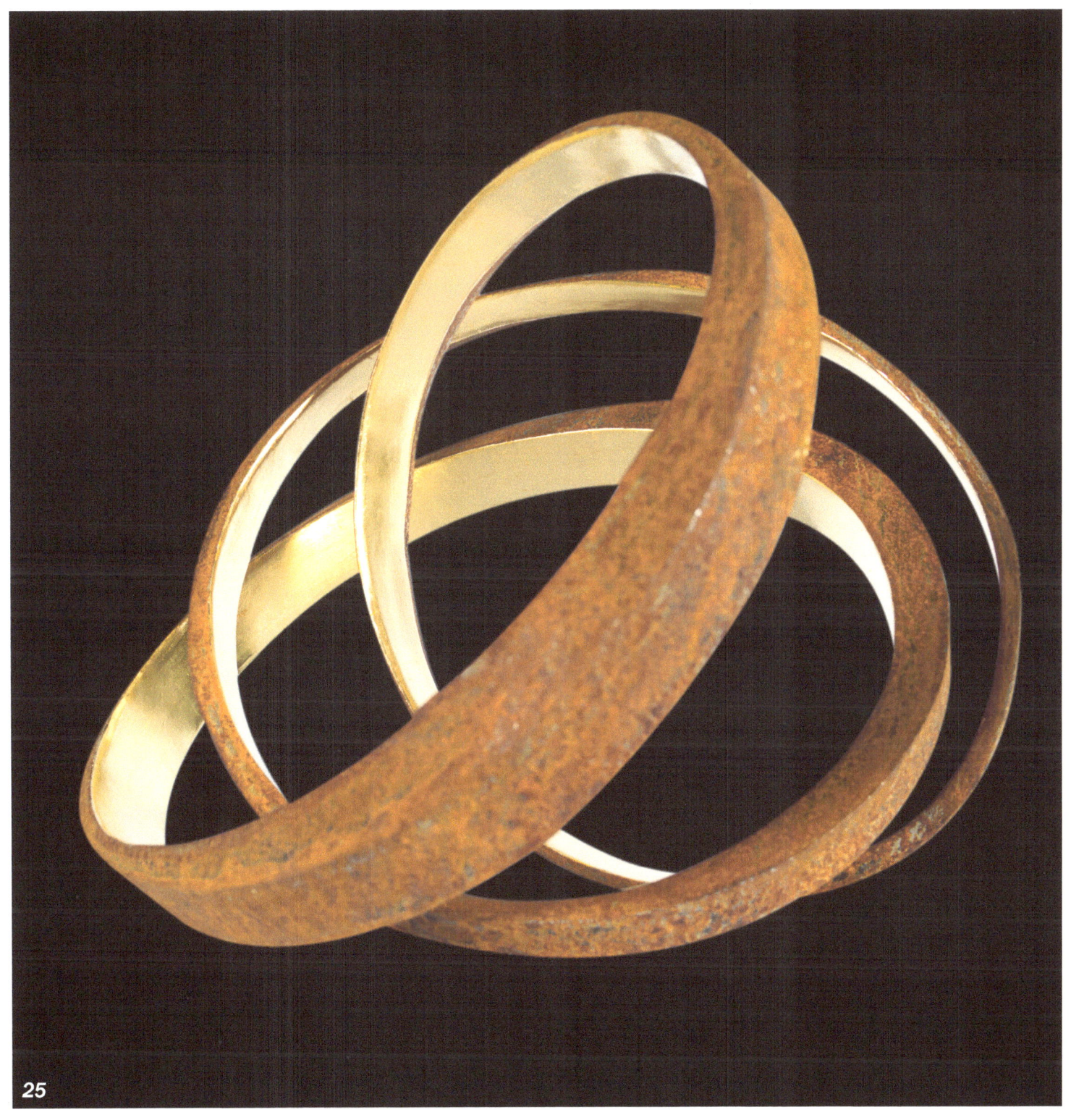

Julie Moselen: Resumé — Recent Commissions & Exhibitions

December 2022	*Seven Sculptors group show. Corban Estate Arts Cenre. Auckland*
March 2022	*RT Nelson Awards. Wellington.*
February 2022	*Sculpture on the Gulf. Waiheke*
November 2021	*Wisdom of the Ancient One .7m x .7m x .2m Corten Steel. Curtin, ACT, Australia.*
October 2021	*Sculpture on the Shore (Online Exhibition)*
June 2021	*Continuum II 1.2m x 1m x .8m Corten Steel. Waiheke.*
April 2021	*Small Sculpture Awards 2021 Winner of the Benefactors Award. Waiheke, Auckland.*
October 2020	*Whenua Pupuke 2.2m x 2.2m x .45m Corten Steel. WDHB North Shore Hospital, Auckland.*
January 2020	*In the stillness between 4m x 2m x .8m Corten Steel, 23ct Gold. Mangawhai.*
October 2019	*Repose 3m x 3m .3m Corten Steel. Waiheke.*
February 2019	*Sunflowers 1.6m x .8m x .6m Aluminium. Taupaki Kindergarten, Auckland.*
November 2018	*Sculpture on the Shore. Takapuna, Auckland.*
October 2017	*National Printmaking Exhibition Mairangi Arts Centre, Auckland.*
September 2017	*Waitakere Trusts Art and Sculpture Awards. Corbans Estate Art Centre, Auckland.*
February 2017	*Solo Exhibition 'Periphery' Railway Street Gallery, Newmarket, Auckland*
October 2016	*Parts of a whole 2m x 1.2m x 1m Oameru Stone. Kumeu Arts Centre, Auckland*
1998	*BA (Hons), Metalcraft and Jewellery Design, Chilterns University, Buckinhamshire, England*
1995	*Foundation Studies in Art and Design, Falmouth School of Art, Falmouth, England*

PAGE	NARRATIVE
4	This is a selection of Julie's jewellery. Some of the themes of this work, such as contrasting textures and surface treatments, are carried through to her present sculpture. Julie has always regarded jewellery as small-scale sculpture, and this is reflected in the detail of her jewellery.
5	Julie's first real sculpture, in Oamaru stone, has special significance in her body of work, for the timeless elegance of it's form.
6	This is Julie's first large scale scultpure. Using a ton of Oamaru stone, this work stands approximately 1.5m in height.
7	The timeless elegance of marble is demonstrated to great effect in this sculpture completed by Julie. The soft, smooth finish of the marble is honed to a soft translucence in the centre of the work.
8	Using a plasma cutter, Julie carefully traces the outline of her patterns on corten steel, creating all the individual pieces that comprise the finished work.
9	Julie's first completed steel sculpture was a massive 2.2m tall, shown here under construction in her workshop, with the outline demonstrated by the side plate temporarily fixed to the wall.
10	Once cut, the metal needs to be bent to conform to the shape of the sculpture. Here Julie is making the most of simple tools to create the organic curves in this piece.
11	Once they have been cut, and shaped, the metal pieces are seamlessly welded into the sculpture. Julie uses MIG and TIG welding, depending on the application, in her work.
12	Following the completion of the structure of the work, the welds are ground to a fine finish. It is during this grinding stage that the work finally begins to take on it's final shape and finish.
13	Many of Julie's works feature the application of a gold leaf surface, creating a stark contrast with the dark, rustic appearance of weathered corten steel.
14	This is the first steel sculpture completed by Julie, named "Wisdom Of The Ancient One."
15	This is another sculpture by Julie, commissioned for the Whenua Pupuke Clinical Skills centre at North Shore Hospital, Auckland.
16	"Repose" is a work by Julie, now in a private collection, that reflects a narrative of continuity.
17	"In The Stillness Between" offers a prescient glimpse of themes that Julie has returned to — the contrast between light and shadow, masculine and feminine, old and new are shown to great effect in this work, now part of a private collection.
18	This sculpture reflects Julie's growing skill and confidence, and represents the realisation of sketches she started creating more than two years earlier. Called "Continuum Amplas," this work was exhibited at the Sculpture On The Gulf exhibition, and is now part of a private collection.
19	Continuum on display during the 2022 Sculpture On the Gulf exhibition. © Peter Rees Photography

NARRATIVE (Continued)

PAGE	
20	Julie's studio at Corban Estate Arts Centre is where she conceives and executes all of her work, using a combination of techniques and tools, some of which she created herself,
21	This is another piece that draws on the themes of "Continuum" at a smaller level of scale.
22	Called "Ballance II," this was one of the series of works that followed the theme of Julie's original sketches. It's more compact and robust proportions reflect a different level of energy.
23	On display during the Corban Estate Arts Centre 20th Anniversary Exhibition, this is the first expression of a new theme. Based on the menhirs and ancient monuments of ancient Cornwall, this sculpture offers a dynamic play on light reflected within it's gold surfaces.
24	"Helix I" represents the unfurling ever changing journey of life, the twists and turns of continual growth, joy and suffering, balance and harmony.
25	Also fabricated from 3mm thick Corten steel, with 23 karat Gold applied, "Presence II" evokes the warmth of the light of the soul, the generosity of spirit and the acuity of intuition, contrasting sharply with themes of age, fragility and degradation.